WITHDRAWN

SAVING
the
LIBERTY BELL

by MARTY RHODES FIGLEY
illustrations by KEVIN LEPP

HUNTINGTON CITY-TOWNSHIP
PUBLIC LIBRARY
200 W. Market Street
Huntington IN 46750

WITHDRAWN

WITHDRAWN

On My Own

HISTORY

Carolrhoda Books, Inc./Minneapolis

The author would like to thank Joshua A. Fink, head tour guide and historian for the Liberty Bell Shrine Museum in Allentown, Pennsylvania, for the kind assistance and excellent insights he offered while she was working on this book.

Photograph on page 47 courtesy of EyeWire by Getty Images.

Text copyright © 2005 by Marty Rhodes Figley
Illustrations copyright © 2005 by Kevin Lepp

All rights reserved. International copyright secured. No part of this book may be reproduced, stored in a retrieval system, or transmitted in any form or by any means—electronic, mechanical, photocopying, recording, or otherwise—without the prior written permission of Carolrhoda Books, Inc., except for the inclusion of brief quotations in an acknowledged review.

This book is available in two editions:
Library binding by Carolrhoda Books, Inc., a division of Lerner Publishing Group
Soft cover by First Avenue Editions, an imprint of Lerner Publishing Group
241 First Avenue North
Minneapolis, MN 55401 U.S.A.

Website address: www.lernerbooks.com

Library of Congress Cataloging-in-Publication Data

Figley, Marty Rhodes, 1948–
    Saving the Liberty Bell / by Marty Rhodes Figley ; illustrations by Kevin Lepp.
      p.   cm. — (On my own history)
    Summary: Recounts how Johnny Mickley, an eleven-year-old boy, helped his father to keep the Liberty Bell safe from the British during the Revolutionary War.
    ISBN: 1–57505–589–9 (lib. bdg. : alk. paper)
    ISBN: 1–57505–696–8 (pbk. : alk. paper)
    1. Liberty Bell—Juvenile literature. 2. Philadelphia (Pa.)—History—Revolution, 1775–1783—Juvenile literature. 3. Mickley, Johnny—Juvenile literature. [1. Liberty Bell. 2. Philadelphia (Pa.)—History—Revolution, 1775–1783. 3. Mickley, Johnny. 4. Revolutionaries. 5. United States—History—Revolution, 1775–1783.] I. Lepp, Kevin, ill. II. Title. III. Series.
F158.8.I3F54 2005
974.811'03—dc22   2003014462

Manufactured in the United States of America
1 2 3 4 5 6 – DP – 10 09 08 07 06 05

For my husband Paul, whose own special creativity, kindness,
and support help me write each book
—MRF

"Giddyap!"

Eleven-year-old Johnny Mickley
flicked the reins of his father's horses.
He was excited to be on the road
to Philadelphia.
This morning he would see
the capital of the American colonies.

Johnny lived with his family
in Northampton Town, Pennsylvania.
Once a month, his father
brought farm goods to the city to sell.
This time, John Mickley had asked
his son to come along.

ESS JULY 4 1776

States of America

American leaders had gathered
in Philadelphia the year before.
They met to decide the future
of the colonies.
The American colonies were ruled
by the king of Great Britain.
But many colonists no longer wanted
to take orders from a king.
In Philadelphia, the American leaders
signed the Declaration of Independence.
The Declaration told the world
that America wanted to be free.
Americans were fighting a war
for their independence.
Johnny wished he could fight too.
He wished he were a hero
instead of a farm boy.

Johnny's father took over the reins
when they arrived in Philadelphia.
The city's streets bustled
with fancy people and plain people.
John Mickley pointed
to a big brick building.
"That's the State House, lad," he said.
Johnny heard the ringing
of a huge bell.
It was Old Independence,
the State House bell.
Johnny listened proudly.
The bell had rung the year before,
on July 8, 1776.
It celebrated the first time
the Declaration of Independence
was read to the American people.

Johnny helped his father
deliver their load of farm goods.
Then they drove the empty wagon to an inn.
Johnny and his father would begin
their long ride home the next morning.

Suddenly, a man stepped quietly
out of the shadows.
He pulled John Mickley aside
and whispered to him.
What did this stranger want?

When the stranger left,

John Mickley returned to his son.

Then he leaned in close to Johnny.

"I have some important business, lad.

Meet me in front of the inn

at four o'clock."

"What's happening, Father?"

asked Johnny.

John Mickley lowered his voice.

"There has been a change in plans.

We will leave Philadelphia

this afternoon."

Johnny started to speak.

But his father pressed one finger

to his lips.

He left without another word.

Johnny sat outside the inn
and watched the people walk by.
He listened for the city bells
to chime the hour.
He wanted to hear Old Independence
ring again.
But no bell sounded.

At last he saw his father with the wagon.
It was filled with a big stack of hay.
Johnny ran out to the street
and scrambled onto the seat.
"Father, why are we carrying this hay?"
Johnny asked.
John Mickley pressed his finger
to his lips once again.

Silently, they rode past tall brick houses.
All the shutters were tightly closed.
They rode beside many other wagons
leaving town.
The wagons were loaded high
with people's belongings.
After a while,
Johnny's father began to speak.

The British army was about
to capture Philadelphia, he said.
General George Washington's army
had tried to stop them.
But the British army was too strong.
People were fleeing the city.
"What will the British soldiers do when they
get to Philadelphia?" Johnny asked.
"Nothing good," said John Mickley.

John explained that the British planned
to melt down Philadelphia's bells.
They wanted to use the metal
for muskets and cannonballs.
"But you and I will help stop them,"
said John Mickley.
Johnny stared at his father.
John Mickley smiled
and winked at his son.
Then Johnny turned around
and stared at the mound of hay.
"Is a bell under there?"
His father nodded.
"The most important bell in the country,"
he said proudly. "Old Independence."
Johnny shivered with excitement.
The famous bell was in *his* wagon.
He was going to be a hero after all.

Johnny and his father
were almost out of the city.
Then they heard the sound
of galloping hooves.
Johnny saw his father stiffen.
Two horsemen rode up to the wagon.
They were British soldiers.
Johnny stared straight ahead
as they passed by.
They never gave the farm wagon
a second look.

Evening drew near.
Other farm wagons joined the Mickleys.
They were hiding bells too.
All of them were headed
to Northampton Town.
The small town would be
a good hiding spot.

Frederick Leaser was
the Mickleys's neighbor.

He drove one of the wagons.

He pulled up beside the Mickleys.

"The British are patrolling this area,"
he warned.

John Mickley thought for a moment.

"Let's take back roads," he said.

"We can meet up again when it's safe."

"I'll tell the others," said Farmer Leaser.

"Godspeed!"

Johnny and his father rode
through the dark woods alone.
Johnny kept a lookout for British soldiers.
Every sound and movement
made him jump.

"Father, what will happen
if the British catch us?"
"They won't, lad,"
John Mickley said.
Then Johnny heard a sound
from the trees.

"Who goes there?" someone shouted.

Two British soldiers appeared

in the distance.

They were coming toward the wagon.

All Johnny could think about

was the bell.

They would find it!

He had to help.

Johnny grabbed the reins.

"Pretend you are sleeping, Father."

Johnny knew the soldiers would ask

a grown man questions.

But they might leave a farm boy alone.

The taller soldier came up to Johnny.

"Look, a wee babe is driving,"

he teased.

"What are you doing on this back road?"

he asked.

Johnny tried not to notice the sweat

trickling down his back.

He tried not to notice

the goose bumps on his skin.

"I must have gotten lost, sir."

he said in a calm voice.

"I was letting my father rest."

The soldiers laughed.

"Turn around," one of them said.

"The main road is a mile to the south."

"Yes, sir," said Johnny.

Johnny made himself drive slowly

toward the main road.

He didn't want the soldiers

to think he was afraid.

John Mickley opened his eyes.

They twinkled with pride.

"That was quick thinking, lad.
I do believe you are a brave one.
You are doing a good job of saving
that bell all by yourself."
Johnny sat up straighter.
He felt like a hero.

Johnny and his father finally rejoined
the other farmers carrying bells.
A cold rain began to fall.
Johnny pulled his jacket close.
At last, they came to the top
of a muddy hill.
Johnny looked down
on an amazing sight.

A huge wagon train was moving
on the road below.
Farmer Leaser caught up
with the Mickleys.
"We're safe now," he said.
"That is part of General Washington's
Continental Army.
We can travel with them."

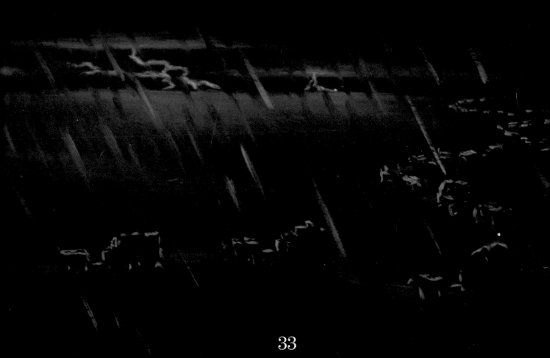

Johnny and his father joined
the army wagon train.
The soldiers told Johnny about
the battles they had fought.
They told him how they worked together
to fight for America's freedom.

Johnny had worked hard too.
He was helping to save
Old Independence.
He could hardly wait to get home
with the famous bell in his wagon.

HUNTINGTON CITY TOWNSHIP
PUBLIC LIBRARY
... Market Street
Huntington, IN 46750

After five days, the wagon train reached
a town called Bethlehem.
Northampton Town was just hours away.
The Mickley wagon made it up
a steep hill to the edge of the town.
Then Johnny heard a loud crack.
The wagon jolted to a stop.
Johnny jumped down
and tried to calm the horses.
His father shook his head.
"The wheel is broken," he said.

"We won't be able to carry the bell any farther."
He called to Frederick Leaser.
He asked his neighbor to take the bell
on to Northampton Town.
Disappointment washed over Johnny.
"Can't we fix the wheel tomorrow?" he asked.

"Then we can take the bell
to Northampton Town ourselves."
John Mickley shook his head.
"It's too risky, lad.
A British spy could be in this town.
Old Independence must be hidden tonight."

Johnny couldn't stop the tears
from filling his eyes.
They would go home
with a wagon full of hay.
What kind of hero would he be?
John Mickley squeezed his son's arm.
"Take heart, lad.
Things will turn out."
The men moved the heavy bell
to Frederick Leaser's wagon.
Johnny couldn't bring himself
to watch it rumble away.

Johnny and his father fixed their wagon.
They rode toward Northampton Town
the next day.
But John Mickley did not head
toward their farm.
Instead, he turned toward town.

"Where are we going, Father?"
Johnny asked.
"You'll see," said John Mickley.
Then they pulled in front
of the Zion Reformed Church.
"I have something to show you,"
Johnny's father said.

Reverend Blumer opened the church door
when they knocked.
He shook both their hands
and smiled at Johnny.
"Old Independence is safe,
thanks to you and your father."
Reverend Blumer bent down.
He pulled up some floorboards.
Below the church floor was the great bell.
Its bronze metal shone softly.
Johnny could make out
the writing on the bell.
He read the words aloud.
"Proclaim Liberty throughout the Land."
Reverend Blumer patted Johnny
on the back.
"The bell will return to Philadelphia
when we win our independence.

Because of you and your father,
it will ring for freedom again."
Johnny touched the bell one last time
before it was hidden away.

Johnny and his father hadn't brought
the great bell to its hiding place.
But they had helped it on its journey.
One soldier couldn't win the war.
One boy couldn't save the bell.
But if everyone worked together,
Johnny knew that one day
America would be free.

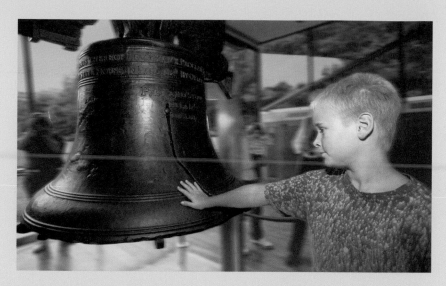

Afterword

The bell that was called Old Independence in Johnny's time is known today as the Liberty Bell. Ten other bells from Philadelphia were hidden with the Liberty Bell in Zion Reformed Church in September 1777. Colonel Benjamin Flowers had been given the job of removing the bells from Philadelphia and taking them some place safe. He asked farmers to secretly carry the bells out of the city in their wagons.

It is most commonly believed that the Mickleys drove the Liberty Bell out of Philadelphia and then handed it over to Frederick Leaser when their wagon broke. But some people believe that Frederick Leaser drove the bell from Philadelphia.

A plaque about the Liberty Bell can be found at the Liberty Bell Shrine. The shrine is in the basement of the

Zion Reformed Church in Allentown (formerly Northampton Town), Pennsylvania. The plaque describes the roles that John Mickley and Frederick Leaser played in the saving of the bell. It tells a story much like the one you read in this book. We know that 11-year-old Johnny Mickley rode with his father on that trip to Philadelphia. However, young Johnny's role on that journey is unknown. We can only imagine his part in the bell's rescue.

The Liberty Bell was returned to Philadelphia near the end of the Revolutionary War. On October 24, 1781, it rang after the American victory in the Battle of Yorktown. That battle ended the Revolutionary War and freed America from British rule.

The great bell continued to ring for important events until it cracked on July 8, 1835. It rang for the last time to celebrate George Washington's birthday on February 22, 1846. The Liberty Bell is on display at Liberty Bell Center near Independence Hall (formerly the State House) in Philadelphia. It remains one of our most beloved symbols of America's freedom.